TERRA

The first boy came from the ocean.

Son two crawled through the *o*

in her signature.

My sister arrived just after him,
looking like she'd been pelted by a storm.

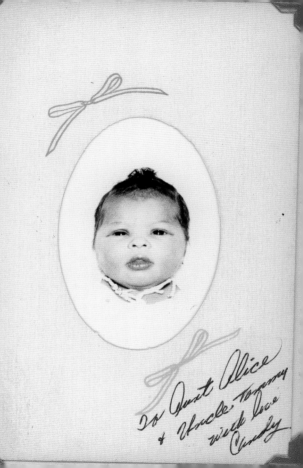

To Aunt Alice
& Uncle Tommy
with love
Cindy

Then another sister both came

and didn't come. The body arrived

but she went elsewhere. *Where?*

I snuck in next, taking up home

inside her salty red grave,

and here I became alive and suspicious.

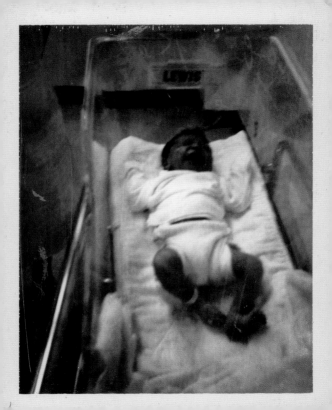

TO THE REALIZATION
OF PERFECT HELPLESSNESS

ROBIN COSTE LEWIS

 Alfred A. Knopf   New York   2022

how can I say things that are pictures   I am not separate
from her   there is no place where I stop   her face
is my own and I want to be there in the place where her face
is and to be looking at it too   a hot thing

TONI MORRISON

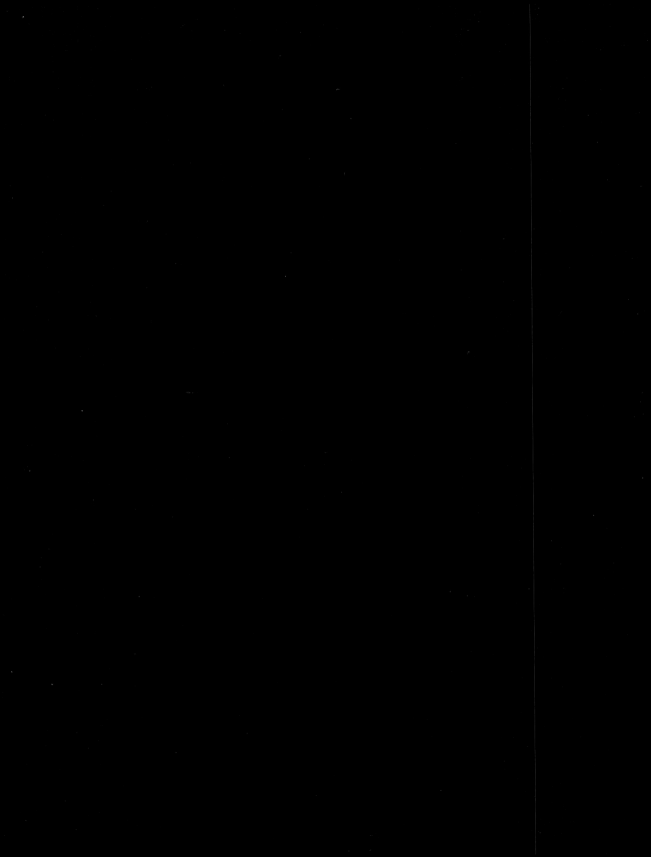

I

I think they thought—

at some point—that

I would come back home.

I think

I thought

so, too.

Do the tambourines miss us?

Signs and marks

    and nothing

        with which to apprentice them.

Evolution—

    the migration

        of imagination—

the image just

    illusion: a profound, prehistoric

        technology of leaving.

Minute anchors,

      something to hold on to,

         not rational—

a private moment, no air—

      the evolution of human beings

         making marks,

the paintings watching us—

an army of black

holes advancing.

The very, very first

person—the very first

human being.

The ones who crossed over long before the Ice Age—

before the last three ice ages—

before the ones before that, too.

Must we see

ourselves

in the water?

Must

the water

be *still*?

(The bar

is lower than

the broom)

My Beloved Husband Lloyd

And didn't we know all this

was going to happen?

Didn't we feel it—all

those decades ago—

standing together talking

on the sidewalk?

I remembered you then,

not from the past, but from

a bright inkling

inside my body

that some would later call *the future.*

Some part of me expected you, knew

you would arrive—faceless,

open, hungry. And how the words felt

then, in our mouths—

all those small-minded Englishes we refused

to speak—all the countless

Blacknesses we could.

The body was the archive.

Desire was our breastplate.

There was a well-known Derg saying once:

To catch the fish, you dry the sea.

You were only four—then—running

along the bottom of the ocean. We were running underwater

toward each other in the opposite direction.

Land was secondary. I was four, then, too.

(A history of alienation perhaps)

(Perhaps I just needed to take

the future off the table)

Devotees of Black

Absence—Disciples

of the Immeasurable.

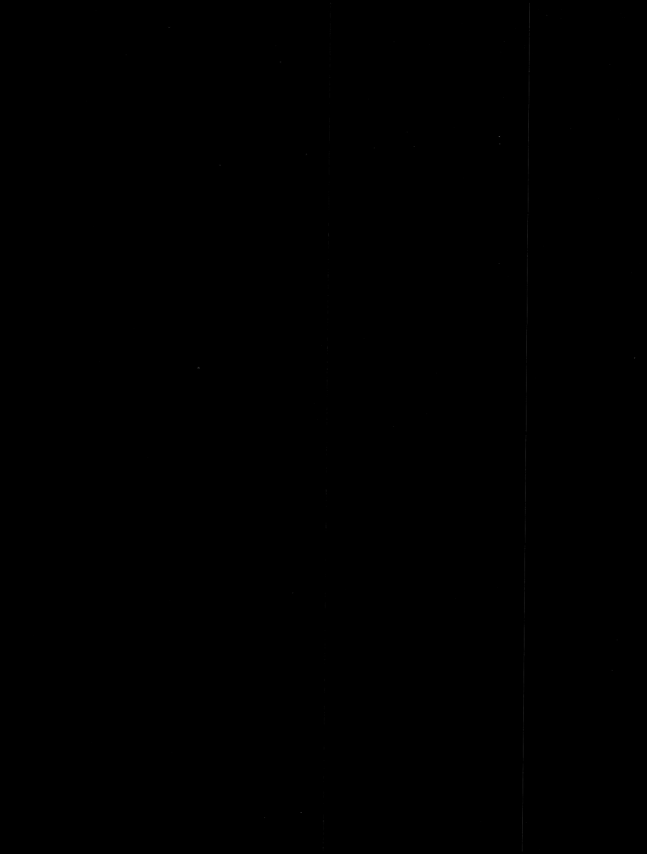

I don't want to be found.

Like the ochre paint you left for me

sitting and waiting inside

an abalone shell 73,000 years ago—

Time: a little girl—

    running backwards—

        wearing a bark dress.

What—then—is *a moment*?

Embodiment: when

there is no other word

to say but *yes*.

Yes

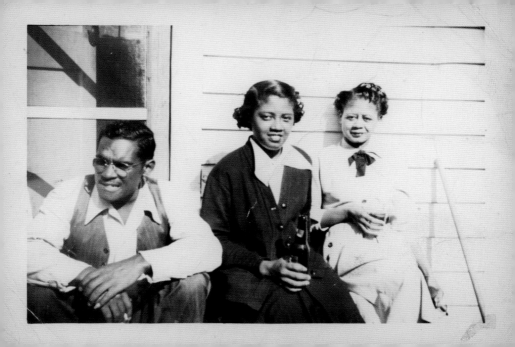

Intimacy—cell to cell.

Do you ever wonder who made the first brick?

The first needle?

The first spoon?

I was on the Ark with you.

I was the hull.

I was the flood, too.

ely, every morning, after a night

of lucid insomnia, my first thought is alw

the same: *Fourteen billion years—*

planet began fourteen billion years ago.

I just lie there.

Thinking.

Presenting

Baby *Robin Kelly Lewis*

Born at *White Memorial*

On *10/15/64* Time *8:06 P.M.*

Weight *2* Lbs. *7* Ozs.

My Parents

Barbara &
Henry Lewis

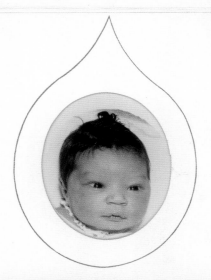

to see everything

that has taken place until

I arrive at the present moment—me

lying in my bed.

Lately, I think about all of the other humans—

now extinct—whose DNA spirals

inside of our own DNA.

Then I remember

that we will one day—soon—be extinct, too.

Fourteen billion years.

I am terrified by the idea

of my own death, but my cells scoff

Sometimes, instead of going

forward, I try to go farther back—

beyond fourteen billion years.

I try fifteen billion, sixteen

billion, sixty billion—long before

our planet was ever created.

Sometimes, the small girl in me wonders

if all of our universes are a roux roiling inside

a large stone cauldron,

inside the warm midnight-blue

kitchen of the infinite Black Sorceress

alive inside my cells.

(Sometimes, I can't stop thinking

about the fact that before Mao Zedong became a genocidal

murderous lunatic, he was—first—a librarian)

ıantum entanglement.

       Something female inside me knows

              that she is evolutionarily expected

 wake up in the middle of the night

      and stare through the dark. And wonder.

            All the worlds spinning beneath me. Togglin

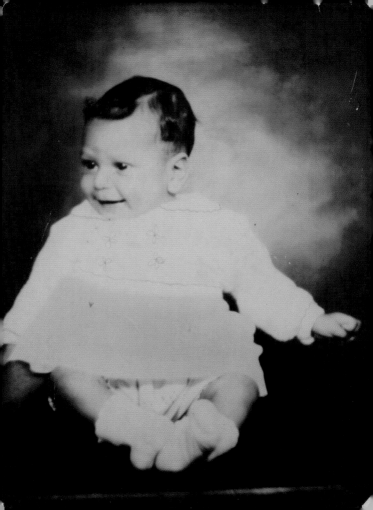

again today,

as I do—

so often—think of you,

wondering

if people can see the sky

of our childhood

the way we still see (the sky)

whenever we think

of each other.

Well, not see, but feel—

the way

There are days

    when all I want

        is to hold your hand

and walk down Wilmington—

    two girls who can feel

        all the galaxies inside

and no one

    to understand—

        or even fathom—that

sprinted far past them; that

while they insist

on our drawing

and redrawing the first

three letters of the alphabet, that

we—like all the other children here—can already see

the planet's arc and all Her

invisible, perfect geometries

(of which you and I

sitting here—now

White space.

Black stars.

To
Daddy

I am sharpening

my arrows, naming each point

after the dead.

The only language

I have is

Language.

McDonogh 36 School nov. 12, 1954

Cafeteria

Like the ancient technology

a scientist discovers in the interior

design of a fossil shell

and then replicates in a factory—a shape

and function that makes a whole industry turn.

That is *pleasure.*

40,000 years ago: there wasn't a continent that had not borne our footprint.

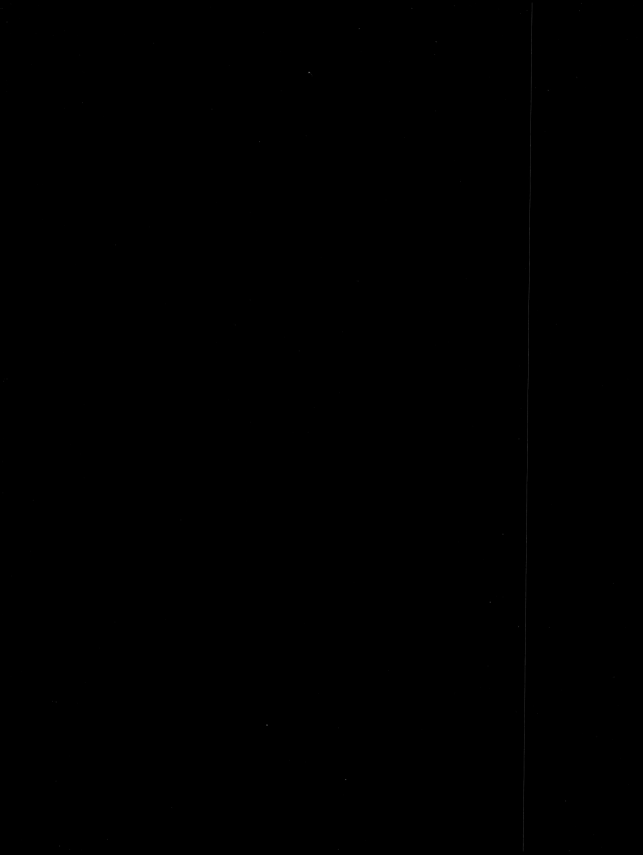

The Mother.

The Daughter.

The Holy Spirit.

Holy Rascal.

my Second Baby

First

Teacher—

Sacred

Door.

BARBARA Rose GRAY
4 1/2 yrs old

To my daughter Robin
Hope you will cherish this
photo of me forever.
Always love
your mother

The way that women fold out

into the universe. The way it folds back

into us. The way we disappear. And reappear.

The way we hide our feathers.

The way we swallow our beaks.

The way we bite down.

Sod and Falsin

The way love says *no*.

The way it sometimes whispers: *Yes.*

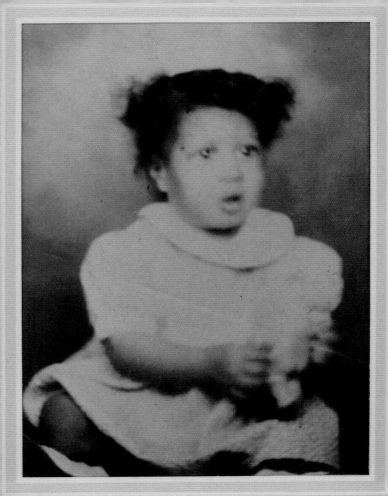

The way a woman steps

toward me, and her steps pry me open.

The way—if I look into her—she steps back.

The question always Black.

HONORABLE DISCHARGE

The way we open, the way

we close—too

soon, too late.

And then reverse it:

the way we close too soon—

and open way, way too late.

The old stories still

    alive inside us, the old ways just

        waiting—a gardenia

corsage, a pearl

    engagement ring, swinging

        my T-strap to and fro—your arm

around me—sitting on a park bench

    together—that very first time

    we saw the sea.

CLEO BROOKS
Swing Stylist Torch and Risque

The way that I can never leave.

And still

stand

in wonder.

The night.

The day.

Cuties 1942

The way I went to sleep with one face,

then awoke the next morning

with another.

The way you walked into our room

and said nothing—never mentioned it.

The way you still recognize me.

The way we rode

through that ancient desert that night,

hour after hour—

the lush and endless darkness. The way

our eyes knew to adjust to the black.

The way—because of the pitch—we began (finally) to see.

The way we held each other's hands.

And the kind men who drove us in their Jeep

(Your father had died). And the stars. The stars.

The way that Time keeps knocking

on my bedroom door. The way that Death lets her in.

The way that Life pours the tea.

Only Love can wear the crown.

I want to see everything.

I want to step inside once again.

(We wish for maps that have never existed, that will never exist)

I touch myself with history.

And there is reason

for great caution when

in the company of paragraphs.

Class
of
1951

All Saints School

The house:

        a parking lot

The tree:

        a wall

The foundation:

        pickpocketed by God

The self:

        soot

Turn the ocean on.

My body a constantly ripening orchard seen only by satellites.

(And yes, it is possible to be

in ecstasy while burning

in hell)

Just be here

with me

on this page.

(Do the tambourines miss us?)

I am trying

to make the gods

happy.

I am trying to make the dead

clap and shout.

II

THE ARK:
SELF-PORTRAIT AS APHRODITE
USING HER DRESS FOR A SAIL

> The effect of such storms of wind
> and snow, or rain, is abject physical terror,
> due to the realization of perfect helplessness.
>
> —MATTHEW HENSON

What makes a child of nine decide to sneak out of his home in the middle of the night and never return? How does a child understand that the world is as much her mother as the human being who gave birth to her? When does the child on the run begin to understand that the body is the womb?

You, Matthew, you.

You step out onto a road in Maryland, 1873. You are nine. Who are you, nine-year-old little boy, hiding behind trees from night riders, tying blankets around your shoes to keep the frost away, walking across a farm at night, knocking at a stranger's door, begging for food?

Your mother, your poor mother. And now your father—dead—too.

Lemuel

Caroline

ii.

Early morning. Still dark. I am in a taxi. The most elegant 'ti Kreyol in the world is on the radio. I catch a sliver and think how one tiny word can be sacred—an artifact—the only green thing that returns inside the beak.

okra

We stop at a toll. It is just a toll—a toll like any toll—but I am thinking, We are all the children of migrants, none of us come from here. And I wonder if the toll-taker ever imagined that one day it would be this black mask in the back seat, or that red mask on the driver.

The toll-taker smiles. I smile. We all smile. It is nine degrees outside. For a moment I am underwater and can't remember which city I am in. Not Boston, but London, Dublin maybe. Or maybe cities no longer exist. Maybe they are all beginning to shrink away, plane by plane, brick by brick. A woman lying dead on her couch for three years watching television.

And then, perhaps because I am suddenly unsure of which town I am in, or which town I will be in by evening, the thought to pass through my mind next is, And just what is so wrong with being destroyed?

iii.

God bless the cook who answers the back door and offers the child a cot.

God bless that mother who thinks, dusting off her hands, One more mouth under the roof won't matter much.

God bless the man who decides he will teach you everything he knows, and then does— every afternoon—in his cabin on the ship for five years straight.

God bless your first piece of white chalk.

God bless the pregnant black slate.

iv.

A child was found. Buried. In a coffin. A child was found. Someone had placed a mask over her chest. On either side of her body was one man and one woman. Also buried. The child was placed between their legs. At some point between AD 330 and 390, all three were placed together in the Ipiutak graveyard—near Point Hope.

v.

"The earth is currently in an interglacial . . . the last glacial period ended about 10,000 years ago. All that remains of the continental ice sheets are the Greenland and Antarctic ice sheets and smaller glaciers such as on Baffin Island."

"In every culture, the oldest memory is water."

vi.

"Tell me again about the flood . . ."

vii.

"We went to sleep in a village, but awoke in the ocean."

"All the ice suddenly melted."

"The sea rose up and took all the land."

"We'd believed it was just a story old people told to frighten the children."

"A god whispered the warning through a reed in the wall.

A man walking by heard his voice."

"There was a beetle. There was a buffalo. There was a midwife."

"We were told to shape the ship like the belly of a bird."

"We grew fins."

"We hid inside an egg."

"We turned back into clay."

"We sought out those who could control the waters."

"Not wind—we moved the ship with words."

"To make sense of all the death, we convinced ourselves we were chosen."

"We learned to live in trees."

"There was a Great Turtle. We climbed onto her back."

"The raven was our compass."

"We threw oxen overboard as offerings."

"Were it not for the trees' tar, our ship could never float."

"There was a frog. It began to drink all of the water."

"One day, a god got a bellyache and vomited up the sun."

"One day, we found a seashell on the peak of a mountain."

"Then the skylark came back

carrying a leaf of okra."

viii.

One day, I come out onto a street in New York. A very old man is on the sidewalk selling antique maps. I smile. I walk up to him.

"Sir, do you have any of the Arctic?"

His eyes look into mine more deeply now. For one quick second, we make love, the way strangers who are not really strangers—they just have never met before—touch each other deep inside with their eyes.

"Of course I do, Darling," he says in a thick and gorgeous Urdu accent. "But," he hesitates, and holds up his index finger: "I have only one."

We smile at each other. We are suddenly in love, and we understand our whole love affair—from beginning to end—will take place right here, between our words, for only these few moments.

I look at the map. On the small sheet of paper, there are two frames: the North Pole is on top, the South Pole on the bottom. All the water is white. The scattered lands are green. Besides the fine black print, these are the only colors. In large bold letters across the middle of both poles is the word UNEXPLORED.

Later I will think: How like this map I am. The top and bottom of me—both—so unknown. My most essential pivots: uncharted yet toggling in perfect geometry. My heart a country called Greenland, yet always covered in ice. My brain an Iceland, but greener than every sea. Prehistoric elephants embedded beneath my skin, along with carved ivory ornaments ten thousand years old that belonged to me when I was someone's wife during the last ice age. Always something in me freezing harder, while another part insists on melting. And then this equator in the middle of my body—so hot, so lush—I can visit, but only for a day.

I buy the map. It is fifteen dollars. The man and I smile at each other. His face is a whole flock of starlings, which suddenly alights upon me—me, bare winter tree. In one minute, we have lived fifty years together. In one minute, we've had ten children. I've tended a goat and brought him a cup of its frothy milk. He's covered my head with a white muslin scarf, then stood beside me while we cremated my father. We've grown gray together. I have loved his body and mind thoroughly. I say goodbye. I rub red ochre into the middle part of my hair. I throw garlands of marigolds into his casket before the moment closes the lid.

ix.

Jonah ran away once.

God appeared to him one night in a dream, begging him to warn yet another city that if the populace did not change its wanton ways, He would destroy it, brick by brick.

(What is it with this God and His envious struggle with the metropolis?)

When Jonah woke up that morning—afraid—he dressed hurriedly, then ran far down to the sea.

(And yet, how I do adore that feeling of God hot on my heels)

Jonah ran to the shore. God followed him. Then Jonah jumped on board a ship, so God became a terrible storm. He wanted Jonah. So Jonah hid below deck. The crew tried everything. Eventually Jonah confessed. It was his body that must play the sacrifice.

His friends did not want to believe it, but—as friends go, of course—they eventually threw him into the sea. Jonah was then swallowed by a whale. And yet, not until after three days of living inside her belly did Jonah cry out for intervention, dedicating his heart to the Lord. At that moment the whale vomited Jonah out. There was a calm shore. Just waiting there. As it had always been.

Jonah in Hebrew. *Yona* in Tiberian. *Ionas* in Greek and Latin.

In Arabic, his name, *Yunus,* means "dove."

x.

There was another Yunus, another dove, who flew to find land and returned with grass and leaves in his beak. A Sufi dervish from Turkey who lived during the thirteenth century. He was one of the first poets to compose in the Turkish, instead of the usual Persian or Arabic, of his day. In other words, he composed in the tongue of his mother, using the same sharp diction as fairy tales. So beloved is he that, from Azerbaijan to the Balkans, everyone claims to have the honor of harboring his grave.

The mature ones are at sea.
A lover is needed to take the plunge,
A diver to bring up the pearl.

:

We were dry, but we moistened.
We grew wings and became birds,
We married one another and we flew.

xi.

When no one is speaking French, I hear people speaking
French. When no one's speaking Spanish, I hear someone
call out to me in Spanish. In my sleep I hear languages
I have never heard. And answer back.

When the whole landscape is covered
in snow, I see trees covered with moss.
When ice turns a river jagged,
I see lily pads. I see palmetto.

xii.

But there is something about all this that is a hiding—something about the colonial qualities of English that (by its nature) performs meaning but runs away from meaning simultaneously. Like that point in the Arctic, that constant latitudinal moment worldwide, where the trees just stopped growing—that porous border all the Earth's trees simply refused to cross. The birds kept going, but the trees turned around and walked back down.

xiii.

Which is to say, the moment I decided there was no such place as home, or what was once *home* no longer existed, that the continent of my family had been flooded, and the ice on which we had lived and thrived for generations had melted, and everyone was gone; which is to say, the moment I admitted I was living on a vast mass of floating ice—alone—the moment I accepted that, I began to feel better. I was dead, it's true, but I was happier. I stood on the new frozen shore watching the light mingle with the ocean. Everyone had become water. *Land* was a story the old people had told to frighten the little children, to keep us from running off.

xiv.

Besides worms and blood, hunger and hope, what lives beneath our speckled masks?

I ran away, too, Matthew.

xv.

One awkward night—as I was changing into a wet girl—a dream of tremendous serpents, each one at least fifty feet long, more than a foot wide. I was standing in the middle of a vast field. The tall grass reached my new mauve nipples (*Bee stings!* my grandmother had called them, landing a mild slap across my cheek, proud). All around me, hundreds, thousands of gigantic snakes glided along the floor of the field. It was night, but the moon was so bright I could see. Whenever a serpent moved, the grass would bend or break on the spot, falling toward me. I walked quietly. I wore the kind of slip my aunts would wear. I was lost. I could hear them, all their bodies breaking the grass trying to reach me.

And then, far off, I noticed an old gnarled giant oak tree standing still in the middle of the field. All I knew was, *That tree is safe, I must get to that tree.* So I began walking, quietly rolling each foot—heel-toe, heel-toe—so the snakes could not hear me. I walked all night.

xvi.

After hours of walking through the night grass, I made it to the crooked tree. But then, just as I reached up, relieved to rest my hand on a large gnarled branch, the branch swung around. It turned for my face, then lunged toward me, eyes glowing yellow, fangs exposed.

I woke up crying. My mother ran into my room. I don't know why, but I told her the whole dream, while she listened in the darkness. And for reasons I still do not understand, I looked up into her blue freckled face and told her it was time for me to leave home. And she agreed.

xvii.

Under their white fur, polar bears have black skin. It is their blackness that keeps them from freezing. Their bodies are so efficient that, if they run for too long, they overheat and die.

To cool off, they fall onto their backs and raise the black soles of their feet into the air. A long time ago, they did this when they were being hunted. Now they do it when teenage tourists chase them down on snowmobiles. They die from their own heat. And because they are scared.

I saw a photograph once. It was of a polar bear, just its head and skin, split down the middle and stretched taut by thongs threaded in grand meticulous triangular stitches every few inches on a giant rectangular frame. The inside of the skin faced up so the sun could dry the blood. Looking at the polar bear's carcass, I thought two things. One: *That's going to keep a family very warm.* And two: *I bet that's how all the men in my family felt.*

It used to be that one caught a bear with just one body, one knife. One man would maybe catch six or seven bears in one winter. No gun. No trap. Some people used dogs.

First, you unleash one dog. It tears toward the bear. The bear chases it back. Just then you unleash another. Then you unleash yet another. You stand far off, on your sledge, watching. You release another. The dogs surround the bear, snipping and yapping. When the bear grows tired, too tired to fight any longer, you draw out your knife. You coat the blade with ice. And what you think they are saying, Matthew, is that because you are a good person, and because your crew is hungry, this bear had decided to die, to give you its body. It has chosen you.

xviii.

There is no way to prove this, Matthew. But they say, after your mother and father died, your stepmother mistook your body for the world. Not spankings—not like a lioness will swat her cub away sometimes for clawing at her ear—not a small effective sting on the hand, but that she *beat you* beat you, that all the years of her dark and female life had accumulated inside her, and your body was the only safe place in the world she could strike back without retaliation. They say that one day she beat you so badly you could not walk or get out of bed for three days afterward. At the time you were only nine. It was 1873, a cold Maryland winter, Matthew. The moment you could walk again, you folded up newspapers into the bottom of your shoes, tied scraps of blanket around your feet, then tiptoed out of the house one freezing late-nineteenth-century night.

xix.

The scientists of your day believed all that heat from Africa radiating in your blood—
Zulu-Wulu! Tiki-Wiki!—would prevent you from surviving the temperatures of the
Arctic. Because you were so brown and so warm—just like the Inuit—they predicted,
Matthew, that you'd be the first to die. They thought you might implode with flames. So
many coco palms in your blood—so many lions, so many tigers, so many bears.

xx.

When I was a child growing up in a tropical city, I lived inside a pure obsessive terror of bears. All bears really, but the word *grizzly,* or even a picture of a grizzly—even now—still makes my blood freeze. I dreamt of them for years. I'm certain I was mauled in another life. Or perhaps it was this life, when I was a child and was actually mauled by an old man—and that was the only way my three-year-old brain could think for me. I remember the year of its beginnings—a new gingham skirt Grandmother sewed for me one morning—but somehow, I can't remember it ever ending. More like a melting. Gone but still in the water. Or maybe it was how the police would prowl through our neighborhood daily, hurling male children onto their hoods, beating them blue with their black pistols.

Or perhaps it was the way they rolled down our streets in their patrol cars, their rifles aimed straight at our bodies, while we jumped Double Dutch, shooting randomly sometimes—the bullet holes freckling the façades of our homes, spreading year after year, as if our houses had caught a rash. Monarch butterflies, bullet holes, spring geckos (we liked to use the red bullet shells to play hopscotch). Or perhaps it was the giant police helicopters, hovering just above our backyards and patios all those countless nights, their searchlights bright enough to break through our drapes and grope around each dark and private room.

xxi.

Eventually, Matthew, you come back: that remarkable small child you once were, running away on a dark road one night when you were only nine, suddenly one day he just comes back.

When you are an old man, and you can no longer remember why you were waiting, or for whom, or when you have made the wise choice and given up waiting for anyone, and even then—still—no one comes. It begins one day like a mild imbalance, like the growing subtle urge to vomit, you don't know why. But by afternoon you are hanging over the toilet, mouth gaped open like a new bird, dry-heaving. And suddenly, while you are there, waiting for your own body—or is it the other way around, your body is waiting for you?—the child steps forward inside you, that nine-year-old runaway on a dark winter road, bruised and brave, he steps forth from your cold, warm body. An iceberg breaks free, calving. And what finally comes out isn't bile, Matthew, but water.

xxii.

During the nineteenth century, whaling ships caught in deadly storms would throw all their whale oil overboard. The luxurious oil, they believed, would subdue the crashing waves. Sometimes it worked. The sea would grow calm. It meant utter ruin, but a whole ship and crew might be saved.

If I could, I would throw whale oil all over my life. I'd empty every barrel.

xxiii.

And then one day, a day long after I had finally run away (so that I could change privately into a young woman), I dreamt a grizzly was walking toward my neighborhood, looking for me. Except this time, for the first time, instead of spending the whole night running away, waking up in the morning wet and humiliated, I looked at the bear—resigned— and instead began to charge toward it.

The bear ran. I ran after it. I chased it to kill it. And I knew if I caught it, I finally would.

Then my neighborhood changed into the woods and there was a rushing ruddy river. The bear was on one red clay bank and I was on another. It stood there staring at me. I stood on the other bank, in my slip, bent over, out of breath, staring back. Suddenly, it dove for me, this twelve-foot-tall grizzly, it dove right into the river, headed for me.

Except—except—the second it hit the water, every hair of its dry brown fur suddenly spiked white. Beneath the fur there was black skin. When it surfaced, it was a polar bear with large black feet.

I smiled. Then called her "Mother."

xxiv.

Once, it was said: no unrelated woman
shall be touched unless she needs medical attention,

or unless she is drowning at sea.
I used to find these statements bewildering.

Now I find them comforting.
She is an ark in the midst of a flood.

She covers herself with black pitch.
She has already begun to gather

all the animals. Inside her
all the nations. Behind

her clavicle exists
a vast and endless ocean.

And there
she sets sail.

xxv.

I wonder sometimes if being a runaway helped you, Matthew. If stepping out onto a dark winter road in the middle of the night, at nine, somehow changed you, made all those twenty-three years of Arctic and American nights possible? Did sleeping on the cot as a child in the back of that diner's kitchen prepare you somehow for a life at sea? And once you went to sea, at eleven, and no one in your family came looking for you, did that make it easier to leave, and to reach? What was the North Pole after that? You'd already been to your own North Pole—in America, when you were nine.

Once, years after I left home, my father and I were talking on the telephone and I was crying, homesick. He was my favorite human being. When I told him I wanted to quit everything—college—and just come home, he didn't flinch. When I said *home,* he just said dryly, "What for?" When I protested that coming home was more important, he stated what seemed to be the most obvious observation of all:

"Ain't shit here."

I can't tell any longer whether I am sad or satiated. They feel so similar. Both seem to secrete the same results: silence, joy. The bear chased me. I ran into the World's arms. And She caught me.

xxvi.

One night—in the middle of all this—you dream you see a narwhal at the mall. She is inside a dry and empty shallow pool just on the edge of a vacant parking lot, beneath a tall fake palm tree, standing upright on her bent flukes, casually examining the edge of her right fin, as if she's overdue for a mani-pedi.

Once there had been a horn—graceful, luminous—a spiraling ivory spike more than ten feet long, heralding from her mouth. Sacred tooth. But now there is a blunt stump, a dead white trunk in the middle of her face to which someone once took a sword. Shorn. But you can see—beneath her black, massive, blubbered body—these two wide gorgeous eyes: hidden, sunken inside a female face. And the delicious imprint of five breasts. And nine hips. And a story so long it contains just two words: *water* and *clay*.

xxvii.

But sometimes I have set myself down, a sliver of rotten seal meat—not like what I am: a red line, a shimmering rush through history, that one rare stone panned from an icy river in the Klondike.

I don't come from cobblestones—I was born at sea. My hair is not tangled white cotton, nor straight sweet cane. I'm merely what is left of the bridge: gray and decayed broken planks standing up in two erect rows across a vast frozen lake.

My body is a translation. Don't speak to me of trade. Speak to me of the astounding black whale who gave up her life for me. Speak to me of whalemilk. Speak to me of her ribs and the driftwood I found—how I used it all for my roof and my frame.

xxviii.

Every life has its flood, its own private ice age, its cage. Every life has a righteously jealous god that sends complete and ultimate destruction. Everyone feels their iceberg melting, the deluge rising inside the eyes.

Two by two: the prized black stallion that runs along the bottom of my sea. The deft killer whales with their perpetual smiles. The sea otters playing beneath a cliff, where I have sat at daybreak bathing inside a hot sulfur spring. The salamanders, the yellow-and-black-striped caterpillars—thousands—that covered the warm west wall of our house one year. The monarch butterflies that emerged. The donkeys. The curious ponies. The stray dogs we fed sometimes. And that tiny vibrant snake, thinner than a pencil, chartreuse, coiled inside my brown three-year-old palm. A green leaf in my beak.

> *Knot of the water*
> *Water of the master*
> *Headwaters—Water divide*
> *Three waters*
> *Water that feeds the well*
> *Secret water*
> *Water catchment*
> *Water of the womb*

I ran away, too, Matthew.

Ten thousand years from now someone will find me, just like this—just like that three-thousand-year-old man—still running, but frozen solid inside a glacier, brandishing a blade.

xxix.

Even light runs away. Even stars. Even the sun—they say—
hides here (to sleep for half the year), only rising
from bed to sit on the horizon just an hour each day

and sip a cup of black coffee. The animals, too,
all clamber to the top—a pulsing crown of endless
birds and whales—and sleep, and give birth.

Even glaciers, calving icebergs, contract here undisturbed.
Everything trying to run away from us—everything
trying to find rest—the planet's crest a haven, bearing all

the runners' weight. Maybe this is what Einstein felt: the Earth's heft
making a curved blue dent in a bed of space—the globe
a speckled robin's egg, cradled inside a nest of tinnient darkness.

xxx.

Or perhaps—perhaps—I am just an upturned tree, all my roots earth
laden and bare. Perhaps I fell over so I could worship at the altars of birds.

Or I am a harlequin waterfowl, speckled—*black-white, black-white—*
hiding safely in day or night. My eyelids are made of feathers

so dark they throw off an emerald sheen. And here I am—still—at home,
bobbing on top of this endless white sea, batting my lashes

toward every beacon—on any remaining shore—ignited
and burning brightly throughout all the black worlds.

III

The sea was more important now than the shore.

VIRGINIA WOOLF

MIGRATION:

THE SEVENTH MERIDIAN

At my back lay the land of sadness—

Day and night were the same tide—

The moon rose midday.

The sun

rose

at midnight

State of California · County of Los Angeles

MARRIAGE CERTIFICATE

I Hereby Certify that on **May** 8th 19 54

at **Los Angeles (Holy Cross Parish)** California, under authority

of a license issued by the County Clerk of the County of Los Angeles, I, the undersigned,

as a **Pastor - Roman Catholic Priest**, joined in marriage,

Henry Gabriel Lewis and **Barbara Rose Gray**

in the presence of **Woodrow W. Fisby**, residing at **0 - W - 57 St. L.A**

California, and **Daisy C. Fisby**, residing at **848 · W · 57 St · L · A**

California.

Denis J. Falvey
Signature of person solemnizing marriage

A crimson sphere

balanced on the brink

of the world.

Snow-blindness.

Battle Harbour.

Morning Star.

Conditions

were never similar.

No two days were the same. Imagine

gorgeous bleakness, beautiful

blankness—the magnificent

desolation about us.

We took a chance.

We started on April 1, 1895,

with three sledges

and thirty-seven dogs—

We reached Anniversary Lodge

on June 25, with two sledges

and only one dog.

Clear, no wind, temperature

fifty-seven below zero.

The reckoning

of distance,

the lion-like months—

too full of the realization

of our escape

to have much

to say. We came to the almost

solid. We paced off

the miles.

There is no more

Beyond. We went to sleep

with our boots on.

Stay aboard, my sole companion. Stay aboard.

We built temporary

    houses. The boxes

        of our provisions, themselves, formed

the walls. The roofing

    was made

        from makeshifts,

such as sails,

    overturned whaleboats,

    rocks.

We had every experience

except Death.

More than once

we looked

Death

squarely in the face.

Now and then, a moon.

Elevation.

Headlands.

Wind-swept

plains. Ice-covered

waters—life-giving

sea.

Every atom

    a finite piece

        of another star—

what remains

    from preceding

        galaxies.

The ever-victorious willingness.

We utilized the trail

made by preceding parties.

We marched

and marched. Onward.

We forced our way.

Din of whistles. Bells.

Alert attention.

Intelligence. Sagacity.

I am sure we covered the necessary

distance to ensure our arrival at the top

of the Earth.

The whole party together, farther

north than had ever been made

by any other human beings.

As we looked at each other,

we realized our position, and we knew

without speaking that the time had come.

Photographs
of
California

We gave each other

the strong

fraternal grip

of our honored fraternity

and confidently expected to see

each other again.

We are at Cape Good

Point. The night

is coming quickly.

I felt all

that it was possible

for me to feel.

But I have started

for a place, and do not intend to run

back to get a better start.

INHABITANTS

&

VISITORS

My fireside,

My darkline,

My border-dotted

Dwelling.

My own alone,

    My firm open,

        My across the road,

            My gentle permission.

My narrow present

Half-obliterated fringe

Of now—

Golden, luxuriant—

My still-shrill war

Dwelling on parole—

Inhumane bricks amid

The oak copse there.

My discolored emphasis—black,

Blacker than any dusky orb,

Before or since:

My orchard of location.

My-thology

(Prominent. Astounding).

My biography

(Robs and murders

The whole history

Enacted here).

Let Time intervene

The most distinct and dubious tradition:

Saluted—

Standing—

Unoccupied

Election.

My labored lethargy—awake—

My poetry skipping,

My bells rung in hot haste—

Engines fire all together. Fresh sparks.

My ever and anon,

My cooled ardor

Thought concluded.

Speaking trumpets,

Passage in the preface,

The soul's only survivor.

Heir of Burning First Moments.

My gaze—my always—remembered absolutely.

My mere presence,

My dark heaven,

Which could never be burned

Or mounted.

The iron hook

Hangs history

(Once more

on the left).

My earthen descendants,

My sufferance,

My vain form

(Midsummer Man Carrying a Load).

My inquired concern—

A potter's wheel of him,

Clay-and-wheel Scripture:

An art ever-practiced.

Last inhabitants

Of these woods

Before me—

Names with coil,

Civil speech carmine,

Curled up by use—

The last symbol a dim garden overrun

with Roman beggar-ticks.

My dent in the earth,

This site,

These dwellings:

Buried cellar stones—

And strawberries,

Thimbleberries,

Hazel bush,

Chimney nook,

Aunt Hil And friends

Sweet-scented black waves

Where the door was sometimes

The well.

Visible

Fate, free will, fore-

Knowledge absolute. Form

And dialect

Edifying as philosophy.

My Vivacious

Lilac Generation:

The door and lintel and sill

Are unfolding—

Plucked by the traveler,

Tended by children

In front-yard plots

Now standing.

Lone century

Universally thirsty

Making the wilderness

. Blossom like the rose:

Deliver me from a city

built on the site of a more ancient city

whose materials are ruins,

whose gardens: cemeteries.

My season,

    My wanderer,

        My house for a week

            Or a fortnight at a time.

My Great Snow,

    My long-time-buried-

        Without-food. My hole,

            Which the chimney's breath made in the drift.

My house,

    My meandering dotted line—

        Same number of steps—same length—

            Coming and going.

My own deep tracks—

Heaven's own blue—

My deepest appointment,

My plainly erect neck.

Feather-lids, Winged-Brother-

Of-the-Peninsular-Relation,

My nearer approach—

Impatient, Delicate

Twilight.

New perch.

Peace smitten on one cheek—

Notwithstanding the odor of morale

(Church-or-State Haul

Load of Manure.

Large fires

Clear when others failed).

My darkness, my lamp

Through the trees—like the nut its kernel.

Unsuspected faith,

God of Defaced and Leaning Monuments.

Enter Ye,

O World, behind us.

Pledge no institution

whichever way we turn.

Blue-Robed Roof, Mother of Pearl flocks,

Form and dissolve the fable, every

Circular inch. Open its seams.

Long to be remembered.

Expect the Visitor who never comes.

Say, "Remain at eventide,

As long as it takes, long enough

to milk a whole herd of cows."

2 Month

BEFORE

before *Before*

Before the land broke into countless pieces

Before knowledge's irresistible urge

Before the last five great mass extinctions—

when Time's Mother was just a little girl

Before *was* was *is*—

when we were just

one cell, sensitive to light

Before the retina

before the pupil

Before the desire

to see you

walk across a field

Before the first

kiss   Before

light and luck

Before bird-hipped

women   Before the evolution

of the wing

Before the birth of stars—live black matter—

and their bright dark

afterglow

Before transition—before impact—

when the beginning was *The End*

and Tomorrow was our only land

Before even the idea of *then*—

when the World had just begun

to whisper to me

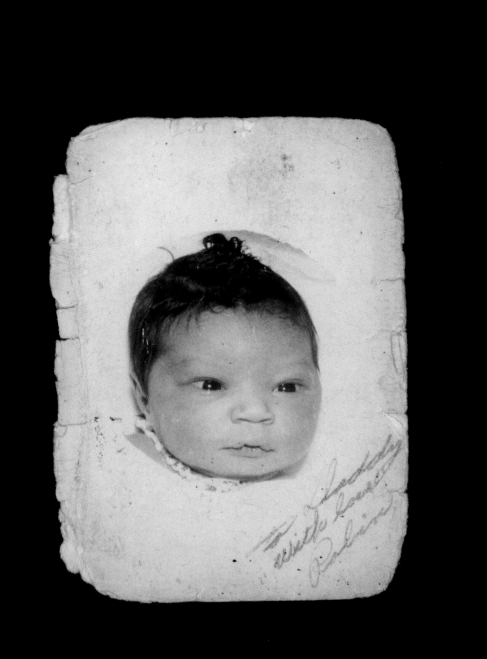

And before

    that exquisite moment

        when you are unaware of me

    watching you—

        just then—right

            before you look up

Tower of Ivory

House of Gold

Ark of the Covenant

Gate of Heaven

Morning Star

Our country is named History

Our Capitol is called Memory

THE EVOLUTION OF SPEECH

Your first word, that

very first time *when*

you first opened

your balmy mouth

toward mine, each red

historical cell leapt

forth, every red syllable

a pulsing wave

from the very first

black galaxy.

You.

And me.

Name Kimberly Griffith
Born at White Memorial Hospital
On October 2, 1955 Time 7:15 P.M.
Weight 8 Lbs. 13 Ozs., Length 20 ins.
Parents Mr. & Mrs. Dion
Griffith Morrow
2 hrs old. (girl)

As a child, I waited

like a bird, open

beaked and excited

for you to give me

the World, word

by word, my mind not blank, just

wide, a map

without names or lines,

sitting blackly—

waiting—my potential

hungry, starving

for all your sign-play.

Name Steven Henry Lawis
Born at White Memorial Hospital
On August 7, 1956 Time 11:34 P.M.
Weight 7 Lbs. 0 Ozs. Length 18 1/2 in.
Parents Barbara & Henry Lawis

_____

_____

To
Grandma & Grandpa
from Stevie

Red axe,

    red dots,

        red iron.

I chewed red.

    Whisked my mouth

        with water *then*

spat over my open-palmed red hand

    onto the red cave wall—

        a royal red trail

which I left just for you

    ninety thousand red years ago—

        so you could talk-talk that walk again.

Prehistoric pillow talk

—offered, received—

we kissed and tongued

through every form

and species

for over sixty thousand generations.

You see me,

don't you?

I see you, too.

We were there.

    We didn't hear

        the first word, *We*

were the first word.

    Not sounds, not grunts—

        black sequence, black syntax,

black adverbs, the first black

metaphor. When I walked

toward you, I was a sentence

speaking. When you looked out

toward my approaching steps, you became

my question mark.

When we spoke words for each other, we

placed all the gods in bondage.

And they liked it.

To *taste,* to *touch,*

to *see,* to *hear,* to *relish*

You.

Everything

we now exchange

will dissolve, disappear.

This eye

with which I look

at you now

will one day

evaporate

again and no

one will ever know

my delight,

how fond I was

of my own pleasure,

of feeling

my aperture

spiraling outward

then in—whenever

you were near. Or

how this tongue

    with all its sublime tastes

        will disappear

(those fresh tuna samosas

    we ate—camels

        sprawled out like commas

between Madagascar

    and Malawi) or *that* kiss—*your* kiss,

        and Tante Mildred's bisque,

or just this: your hand

    raised toward mine,

        offering me a glass.

And those words

you finally found.

And the other words

I found—too—to say

back to you.

All of it

will be

erased, all of it

will never be

recorded

in the fossil record.

And I don't care—

Sept 1968

our black

deep mystery perfect—

you and me—

sitting here—

one hundred

thousand years ago—

without any possibility—

or need—for

documentation.

THE PROCESS

When I reached the ship again and gazed into my little mirror, it was the pinched and wrinkled visage of an old man that peered out at me, but the eyes still twinkled and life was still entrancing. This wizening of our features was due to the strain of travel and lack of sleep; we had enough to eat, and I have only mentioned it to help impress the fact that the journey to the Pole and back is not to be regarded as a pleasure outing, and our so-called jaunt was by no means a cakewalk.

MATTHEW HENSON

Being alone—compelled

to linger—to be created,

to be physical,

to lose purpose

(which is, after

all), to dwell.

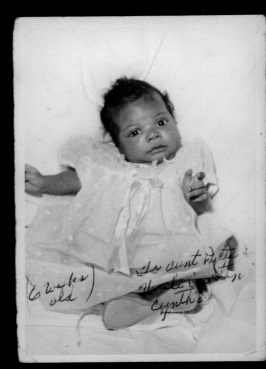

(6 weeks old)

To aunt Mattie &
Uncle Green
Cynthia

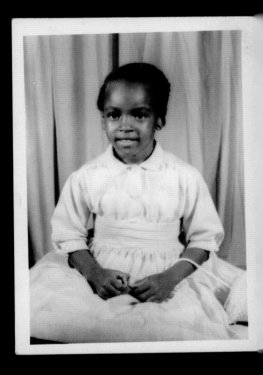

Birth—or Death—

  the fearless eyes

    of mystery,

of any desire. God

  in an attempt to make vivid

    His endeavor—

extreme, universal—

  inescapable correct delusions

    we fall into. Reason

that incorrigible

  Disturber-of-the-Peace, that

    Future-Better-Purpose-

Society chaos—in order

  to make life bearable.

    General Beginning-of-Time

unwilling, indeed unable,

  to live without minimizing

    human damage.

However the mystery

    of being human is stable,

        the answer hides

a breed of honor:

    all-tender

        reality.

Peculiar nature

    never ceases warring:

        for change, for health.

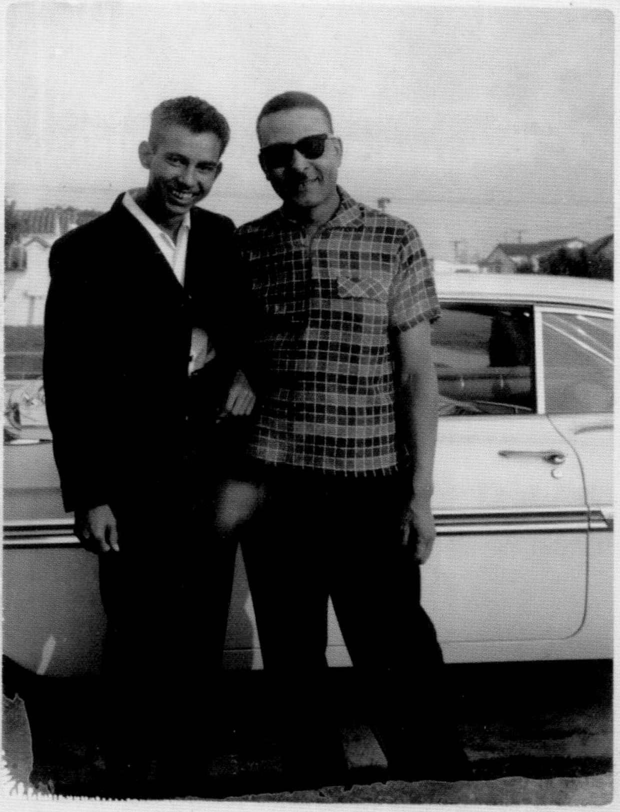

Now: Love.   See

the face, this face,

the most

extraordinary—essentially

rare barrier—frightened

of precarious security.

Delicate,

strenuous.

Unshakeable.

We cannot live

without the danger

of being this

utterly beautiful.

And typical.

And proven.

This continent: Fear—

    one's interior—

        uncharted

chaos—a nation

    modified—

        or suppressed,

History trapped

    in paralysis—unable

        to access weaknesses—

or strengths.

And this: *We*

are strongest—

not for the Reason—

but for the Record

most clearly revealed

in the people.

This war is

a Lover's War.

LANDSCAPE

Pleasure is black.

I no longer imagine

where my body

stops or begins.

Skin transparent. Face

speckled by the spit

of several centuries.

All the borders

stare

at the same fires.

Oh, Mamere,

I'm sorry.

Here I am.

HEAD-TURNER

Orurania	the heavenly one
Pendemos	of the people
Hegemone	leader
Strateia	of the army
Pontia	of the sea
Enoplon	armed
Nomophylakis	guardian of laws
Epistrophia	Head-turner
Charidotes	joy-giver

NAVEL

We crawled out of her navel

one by one, then waited

until we were all here.

That lucid moment when

the last wet child learned to stand,

we began walking.

We walked slowly.

We took some time.

We took more than that.

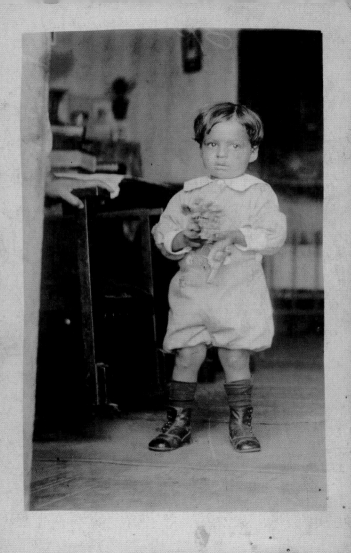

When we began to grow

hungry, some offered to turn

themselves into animals.

Smiling, they said, Here, eat me.

Others turned into water, rivers, trees.

Some turned themselves to dirt

so we could walk a path. We crept

toward the edges, clawed and crawled to the top

of the world, and there we clung.

Instead of a mouth, a woman

spoke through a vibrant yellow

bill. Sometimes we visited the Man

on the Moon, sometimes he let us

inside his house, sometimes

his transparent hollow wife would dance.

Later, when people asked us,

Where did you come from?

We could only answer: *water.*

A whole language comprised

of just one word. We walked

onto the water. We built houses

on the water. We had babies

on the water. We sewed clothes

made of water with needles made of ice.

The night so constant

changed us. The planets

taught us a vocabulary

without any alphabet.

The trees began to walk.

At night, the ocean glowed

green from underneath.

Our roofs were made of whale

ribs, our lamps were stone

that burned clear oil. And now

I've turned my face into this page

so we could sit here together again.

Cousin
Henry
1943

NEW ORLEANS FISH MKT.
213-298-9738

In Loving Memory of

Leontine J. Lewis

Born: February 20, 1900
Died: May 18, 1990

"May thy soul and the souls of all
the faithful departed, through
the Mercy of God, Rest in Peace."
...Amen

1 Jesus
2 Family
3 Money
4 Love
5 good health

It has been
found again.

What has?

Eternity.

—RIMBAUD

Twenty-five years ago, after I phoned my aunt Nani to say I had found a suitcase of old pho-
tographs under my grandmother's bed, she responded clearly, confidently: "Write a book."
I hope this work serves as a reminder to all Diasporic peoples that a century or two of time
is quite short, and that the real histories of our cultural innovations extend back for tens of
thousands of years. As a child of migration, I hope it expresses my deep awe for the deft
imagination of migrants worldwide.

This book is also a tribute to the very specific Black migrations—not north, but *west*—
from Louisiana to Los Angeles, embarked upon during the early twentieth century in the
United States, an homage to the rigorous survival of Diasporic Gulf cultures, languages,
technologies still thriving all along the Pacific rim. My most immediate relatives began leav-
ing Louisiana after the Great Depression and World War II, fleeing the white terrorism intrin-
sic within the failed experiment of American democracy. They transplanted a large vein of
our West Bank culture to Compton and Los Angeles. Three young sisters—my grandmother
Dorothy Mary, her sister Hildreth Louise, and later their sister Eunice Josephine—left their
segregated city alone, carrying only what they could bring in their segregated suitcases on
a segregated train. Their brothers went north to Chicago. Their sister, Myrie, along with
countless other relatives—Tanti Marguerite, Aunt Mildred Lemieux, Leontine Lewis, Elsie
Lewis—remained in our beloved city: New Orleans, where their descendants still thrive
today. Now our relatives number in the hundreds. But were it not for the unfathomable
courage of these three women, and a few of their cousins—Marcella Coste, Theresa Coste,
Bernadine Coste, Eula Johnson, just to name a few—none of us would be here. We owe our
existence to the migrational wisdom and bravery of Black daughters.

Of course, my grandmother and great aunts did not migrate alone. One by one, they also
brought their children along with them: my mother arrived by train while still a teenager.
Her sister and brothers, my aunts and uncles, arrived piecemeal on this train, in that car. So,
thank you, first of all, to my most immediate elders—the brave clan of children who helped
their mothers to shepherd a whole branch of our family west: Carlton Eugene Brooks, Jr.,
Ella Leinani Tsing Keau Chai Brooks, Alice Claire Coste Brooks Johnson, Thomas Starke,
Sr., Dion Griffith Morrow, Sr., and Lydia Evelyn Coste Thomas Morrow. Of these, I am
most especially indebted to my parents, Henry Gabriel Lewis and Barbara Rose Coste Gray
Lewis, who, like all lovers, met accidentally while my father was vacationing, and—thank
God—had the profound courage to say yes to Life. Thank you as well to their descendants,

my siblings and cousins, the first generation born outside of what felt like our own country, Louisiana, and who—like me—were born shortly after our arrival in Los Angeles: Jan Sherri Morrow Bell, Leonce Kawika Soong Yen Brooks, Leontine Malia Ana Tsing Keau Brooks, Ritchie Michael Lewis, Reta Lewis, Steven Harry Lewis, Candice Theresa Lewis Watkins, Cydney Hildreth Morrow, Dion Griffith Morrow, Jr., Lori Ana Morrow, Kimberly Griffith Morrow Wade, Kendall Sebastian Starke, Sr., Thomas Starke, Jr. May we never forget the beauty of what we saw and did--and the untranslatable experience of being loved deeply and blackly.

Most especially I offer endless bright red anthuriums to the well-shod feet of my grandmother Dorothy Mary (née Coste Thomas) Brooks, who told me once that our families in New Orleans didn't starve during the Great Depression because everyone had a vegetable garden. And she had a needle.

Imagine, then, the startling awareness that slowly emerged inside my body: over seven decades, my grandmother, American seamstress, born in 1908, in addition to all else (sewing in New Orleans during the Depression, sewing in postwar Downtown LA factories, sewing clothes on the side, sewing costumes for Hollywood, sewing our school clothes, knitting our socks), not only created and preserved this invaluable archive of Black culture, but she also picked up a camera, then framed the world.

NOTES & ACKNOWLEDGMENTS

The prologue first in appeared in *Lucid Knowledge: The Currency of the Photographic Image/Lucid Knowledge. Fotografie als Währung—zu Aktualität, Relevanz und Verbreitung von Bildern* (Berlin: Hatje Cantz, 2022), edited by Koyo Kouoh, Rasha Salti, Gabriella Beckhurst, and Oluremi C. Onabanjo.

The writing from pages 18 to 161 is an excerpt from an ongoing multimedia collaboration with Julie Mehretu titled *Intimacy.*

Section vii of "The Ark" (pages 171–73) is dedicated to Alondra Nelson.

The poems on page 177 of "The Ark" are excerpted from *The Drop That Became the Sea: Lyric Poems of Yunus Emre,* by Yunus Emre (1240–1321), translated from the Turkish by Kabir Helminski and Refik Algan (Boston: Shambhala, 1999).

"Migration: The Seventh Meridian" is part cento, part lyric, after Mathew Henson's *Henson at the North Pole.*

"Inhabitants & Visitors" is an erasure of Henry David Thoreau's chapter "Former inhabitants; and winter visitors" from *Walden; or, Life in the Woods* (1854). I wrote this piece for Kevin Young on the occasion of his being named the director of the Schomburg Center for Research in Black Culture and to commemorate the opening of the National Museum of African American History and Culture.

"The Process," an erasure of James Baldwin's essay "The Creative Process," is dedicated to Alfre Woodard, with gratitude.

:

Grateful acknowledgment is made to the following publications, galleries, and museums, where a number of these poems and installations first appeared.

"The Evolution of Speech" first appeared as part of a piece entitled "Recursion: Self-Portrait of My Desire as the Evolution of Language in Homo Sapiens," in *Glenn Ligon: Untitled (America)/Debris Field/Synecdoche/Notes for a Poem on the Third World* (Regen Projects, 2017). • "The Ark" first appeared in *Transition Magazine.* • "Navel" first appeared in *Time.* • *Inhabitants & Visitors,* chapbook, Clockshop, Los Angeles. • "The Process" first appeared in *Perceptual Drift: Black Art and an Ethics of Looking,* edited by Key Jo Lee. • Lines from the poem "Landscape" were used as episode titles throughout the fourth season of Ava DuVernay's TV drama *Queen Sugar* (OWN TV: The Oprah Winfrey Network). • *Intimacy,* single-channel video installation in collaboration with Julie Mehretu, Galerie Marian Goodman, Paris. • *Lucid Knowledge,* Triennial of Photography, Hamburg, Germany. • "Black/Queer/Abstract: A Convening on the Occasion of Julie Mehretu," Whitney Museum. • *Inhabitants & Visitors* installation, *Beside the Edge of the World,* The Huntington Museum. • "Migration" was originally performed live with Terrance McKnight, Ava DuVernay's ARRAY Now/Kellogg Foundation's National Day of Racial Healing. • "Navel," text installation, *Water & Power* exhibition, The Underground Museum.

Iron-age gratitude to the following institutions for the invaluable and mysterious gift of time: Guggenheim Foundation; Academy of American Poets/Mellon Foundation; Ford Foundation; Eric Garcetti and the entire staff of the Los Angeles Mayor's Office; City of Los Angeles Department of Cultural Affairs; Cave Canem Foundation; New York University, Creative Writing Program; University of Southern California.

:

I first showed parts of this project, under the title *Lousy Anna,* to the fine faculty at Bard College's MFA program. And while I did not complete the program, my reception there one summer would change the trajectory of this work and my life. I am grateful to Cecilia Dougherty, Ann Lauterbach, Jeffrey DeShell, Matthew Sharpe, Leslie Scalapino, David Levi Strauss, and especially Lynne Tilman.

I would also like to thank my teachers: Nina Payne and Andrew Salkey (Hampshire College Creative Writing Program); Evelyn Higginbotham, Stephanie Jamison, and Cornel West (Harvard Univeristy Divinity School); Denis Donoghue, Deborah Landau, Sharon Olds, Rachel Zucker, and especially Yusef Komuyakaa, who encouraged me to allow my obsession with Matthew Henson to roam freely (New York University MFA in Creative Writing Program); Ann Marie Yasin, Amy Ogata, Vanessa Schwartz, Akira Mizuta Lippit, Mike D'Amato, and most especially Kate Flint (Visual Studies Research Institute, University of Southern California); Marilyn Nelson, Cornelius Eady, and Toi Derricotte (Cave Canem Foundation). Thank you, also, to all the feminist theologians whose research over the centuries has changed the landscape of our psyches with their intellectual rigor and imagination. Your work has helped me learn how to think more clearly, decade after decade.

Most of all, however, I owe my gratitude to the University of Southern California's English Department's PhD in Creative Writing Program, where I have had the privilege of teaching for the last several years. This book would not exist without the inspired championing I've received right next door from my esteemed colleagues: Flora Ruiz, Natalie Hunter, April Miller, Sherry Velasco, Lisa Itagaki, Peter Mancall, Percival Everett, Dana Johnson, Susan McCabe, and Janalynn Bliss. All the magic that happens in our halls happens because of you—most especially my mentor, teacher, friend: David St. John.

Finally, thank you: Andrew Wylie and all the staff at the Wylie Agency, most especially my agent, Jin Auh, who sees a self inside me whom I have yet to meet. My talented studio staff: Javaun Crane-Bonnell, Tinna Flores, and creative director of pre-production, Emily Rose, who gave me the gift of her brain and her hands. And at Knopf: Zuleima Ugalde, Soonyoung Kwon, John Gall, Ellen Feldman, Peggy Samedi, Andy Hughes, Josie Kals, Madeleine Denman, Andreia Wardlaw, Anne Achenbaum, Kathy Hourigan, Matthew Sciarappa, Reagan Arthur, Jordan Pavlin, and, most especially, my editor, Deborah Garrison.

To my friends and family, my gratitude is as black as this page—deep, endless, infinite. Candy Watkins and Sheila Coleman: I'm speechless. And Terra—always.

Within the final year of this book's completion, both my leontine mother, Barbara Lewis (1936–2022), and my voracious mentor of thirty-five years passed away. I think it fair to say that my mother gave birth to my body and heart, while my mentor, Mary McHenry (1933–2021), professor emerita of Mount Holyoke College, was the mother of my mind. I would not have written a word were it not for both of their elegant, intellectual care. This book is dedicated to both, in memoriam.

Also in the course of my completing this book, our longtime publisher and editorial director of Knopf, Sonny Mehta, and Toni Morrison, one of Knopf's greatest writers, both passed away.

All of these are losses from which I hope never to recover.

Subjects in order of their appearance in these pages: page 3: Ritchie Michael Lewis • page 5: Steven Harry Lewis • page 7: Candice Theresa (née Lewis) Watkins • page 9: [Unknown] • page 11: Robin Kelly Coste Lewis • page 19: Heloise Coste (?) • page 21: Alice Claire Coste Brooks, Dorothy Mary Coste Thomas Brooks, Carlton Eugene Coste Brooks, Jr., Barbara Rose (née Coste Gray) Lewis • page 23: [Unknown] • page 25: Barbara Rose and high school friends • pages 28–29: Henry Gabriel Lewis, Steven Harry Lewis, and unknown teammates, Orioles baseball team, Little League, Compton, CA, mid-1960s • page 31: [Unknown] • page 33: Jane (née Taylor) Gonzalez, Kary Kirby Taylor • page 35: "Lloyd" [Unknown] • pages 38–39: [Unknown], Broadway and 8th Street, Los Angeles, CA, Dorothy Mary Coste Thomas Brooks possible photographer • page 41: [Unknown] • page 47: Danny or Tyrone Lewis (?) • page 49: David Thomas, James, or David Jr. Thomas • page 51: Thomas Starke, Jr., Candice Lewis, Kendall Starke, Robin Coste Lewis • page 55: Cornelius Johnson • page 57: [Unknown] • page 58: [Unknown], Barbara Rose (née Coste Gray) Lewis, Kimberly Griffith Morrow, Steven Harry Lewis • page 61: Robin Coste Lewis • page 62: [Unknown] • page 65: (first image) Thomas Starke, Sr., Candice Theresa Lewis Watkins, Kendall Starke, Sr.; (second image) Charles Johnson, Thomas Starke, Sr. • page 67: [Unknown] • page 69: Robin Coste Lewis • page 71: Wardell Johnson, Kirk Johnson, Donna Johnson, Eunice Brown Johnson, Miriam Johnson, Steven Johnson, Aaron Johnson, Wilfred Johnson, Jr., and his dog, Rinnety • page 73: Alice Claire (née Coste Brooks) Johnson • page 75: [Unknown] • page 77: [Unknown] • page 79: Barbara Rose (née Coste Gray) Lewis • page 81: Richard Starke, Thomas Starke, Sr., Alice Claire (née Coste Brooks) Starke Johnson, Barbara Rose (née Coste Gray) Lewis • page 83: Danny or Tyrone Lewis • page 85: [Unknown] and Eunice Josephine (née Coste Thomas) Wheeler • page 86: Alice Claire (née Coste Brooks) Starke Johnson, Wilfred Brown, Jr., Dr. Lucien Lewis, Lily Taylor • page 87: David Merlin Thomas, Jr., Theresa (née Cottles) Lewis, [Unknown], [Unknown], possibly "Uncle Doc" Wheeler • page 89: Barbara Rose (née Coste Gray) Lewis • page 91: Possibly

Griffith Morrow, Jr., Eunice Josephine (née Coste Thomas) Wheeler, Hildreth Louise (née Coste Thomas) Johnson, Dorothy Mary (née Coste Thomas) Brooks, Myrie (née Coste) Thomas • page 263: Dorothy Mary (née Coste Thomas) Brooks • page 265: [Unknown] • page 267: Mary Alice (née Keifer) Johnson, Charles Johnson, Hildreth Louise (née Coste Thomas) Johnson • page 269: Dorothy Mary (née Coste Thomas) Brooks • page 270: [Unknown] Most probably Candice Theresa (née Lewis) Watkins • page 271: Kendall Sebastian Starke, Sr. • page 273: [Unknown] • page 275: [Unknown] and Dorothy Mary (née Coste Thomas) Brooks • page 277: Robin Coste Lewis • page 281: Leonce Kawika Soong Yen Brooks, Dorothy Mary (née Coste Thomas) Brooks, Carlton Eugene Brooks, Sr., Ella Leinani Tsing Keau Chai Brooks • page 285: [Unknown] • page 286: [Unknown] • page 289: [Unknown] • page 291: [Unknown], Steven Harry Lewis, Dorothy Mary (née Coste Thomas) Brooks, [Unknown], [Unknown] • page 293: Robin Coste Lewis • page 295: Lydia Evelyn (née Coste Thomas) Morrow • pages 297–98: Sisters of the Holy Family, 1899 (?) • page 303: Kimberly Griffith Morrow • page 305: Steven Harry Lewis • page 307: Eunice Josephine (née Coste Thomas) Wheeler • page 309: Tante Marguerite Brown, Wilfred Brown, Sr. • page 311: Robin Coste Lewis, Candice Theresa (née Lewis) Watkins, and Compton cheerleading team • pages 314–15: Carlton Eugene Brooks, Sr., Dorothy Mary (née Coste Thomas) Brooks, Barbara Rose (née Coste Gray) Lewis, Alice Claire (née Coste Brooks) Starke Johnson, Thomas Starke, Sr., Richard Starke, Lila Starke, James Earl Starke • page 317: [Unknown] • page 319: [Unknown] • page 321: [Unknown] • page 322: Leonard Alson Thomas, Dorothy Mary (née Coste Thomas) Brooks, Carlton Eugene Brooks, Sr. • page 325: LaRuth (?) • page 326: [Unknown], [Unknown] • page 327: Lucien Lewis, [Unknown] • page 328: [Unknown], [Unknown], Barbara Rose (née Coste Gray) Lewis • page 329: Barbara Rose (née Coste Gray) Lewis, [Unknown] • page 331: [Unknown] • page 333: "Herbie" Hunter (?), Carlton Eugene Brooks, Sr. • page 335: Barbara Rose (née Coste Gray) Lewis, Steven Harry Lewis (?), [Unknown] • page 337: Dorothy Mary (née Coste Thomas) Brooks, LaRuth (?) • pages 340–41: Ritchie Michael Lewis (middle row, center) and team, West Park, Compton, CA • page 345: Miriam Johnson, Wilfred Brown, Jr. • page 347: Cydney Hildreth Morrow, Candice Theresa (née Lewis) Watkins • page 349: Cleo Brooks • page 351: Dion Griffith Morrow • page 355: Alice Claire (née Coste Brooks) Starke Johnson • page 359: Steven Coste Thomas • page 361: [Unknown], [Unknown], [Unknown] • page 363: Dorothy Mary (née Coste Thomas) Brooks, Lydia Evelyn (née Coste Thomas) Morrow • page 365: Barbara Rose (née Coste Gray) Lewis, photo negative • pages 368–71: [Unknown], [Unknown], [Unknown], [Unknown], [Unknown], [Unknown], [Unknown], [Unknown], [Unknown], [Unknown], [Unknown], [Unknown], [Unknown], [Unknown] • page 373: Cousin Henry • page 374: Verso • page 376: Collage: Money order receipt to Robin Coste Lewis from Henry Gabriel Lewis (1988); memory card, Leontine Josephine Lewis; receipt and phone number of New Orleans Fish Market; found list made by Barbara Rose (née Coste Gray) Lewis • page 381: Close-up of Dorothy Mary (née Coste Thomas) Brooks holding a photograph.

A NOTE ABOUT THE AUTHOR

Robin Coste Lewis is the author of *Voyage of the Sable Venus,* winner of the National Book Award for Poetry and a finalist for the Hurston/Wright Legacy Award and the Los Angeles Times Book Prize. The book was named a best book of the year by *The New Yorker* and *The New York Times,* and a best book of the last twenty years by *Literary Hub.* Lewis is also coauthor, with Kevin Young, of *Robert Rauschenberg: Thirty-Four Illustrations for Dante's Inferno.* The former poet laureate of Los Angeles, she holds a PhD in poetry and visual studies from the University of Southern California, an MFA in poetry from New York University, an MTS in Sanskrit and comparative religious literature from Harvard's Divinity School, and a BA from Hampshire College. Her work has appeared in *The New Yorker, The New York Times, The Paris Review, Transition,* and many other journals. Lewis, who has taught at Hampshire College, Hunter College, Wheaton College, and the NYU MFA in Paris, is writer-in-residence at USC.

THIS IS A BORZOI BOOK PUBLISHED BY ALFRED A. KNOPF

Copyright © 2022 by Robin Coste Lewis

All rights reserved. Published in the United States by Alfred A. Knopf,
a division of Penguin Random House LLC, New York,
and distributed in Canada by Penguin Random House Canada Limited, Toronto.

www.aaknopf.com

Knopf, Borzoi Books, and the colophon are registered
trademarks of Penguin Random House LLC.

Library of Congress Cataloging-in-Publication Data
Names: Lewis, Robin Coste, author.
Title: To the realization of perfect helplessness / Robin Coste Lewis.
Description: First Edition. | New York: Alfred A. Knopf, 2022.
Identifiers: LCCN 2022001933 (print) | LCCN 2022001934 (ebook) |
ISBN 9781524732585 (hardcover) | ISBN 9781524732592 (ebook)
Subjects: LCGFT: Poetry.
Classification: LCC PS3612.E98 T69 2022 (print) | LCC PS3612.E98 (ebook)
| DDC 811/.6—dc23
LC record available at https://lccn.loc.gov/2022001933
LC ebook record available at https://lccn.loc.gov/2022001934

Jacket photograph: Dorothy Mary Coste Thomas Brooks Collection
Jacket design by John Gall

Manufactured in China
First Edition